Road Trip: National Parks

GRAND CANYON NATIONAL PARK

BY SANTANA HUNT

Gareth Stevens PUBLISHING

10792480

Please visit our website, www.garethstevens.com. For a free color catalog of all our high-quality books, call toll free 1-800-542-2595 or fax 1-877-542-2596.

Library of Congress Cataloging-in-Publication Data

Hunt, Santana.
Grand Canyon National Park / Santana Hunt.
pages cm — (Road trip: National Parks)
Includes index.
ISBN 978-1-4824-1683-1 (pbk.)
ISBN 978-1-4824-1684-8 (6 pack)
ISBN 978-1-4824-1682-4 (library binding)
1. Grand Canyon National Park (Ariz.)—Juvenile literature. I. Title.
F788.H79 2014
979.1'32—dc23
2014022756

First Edition

Published in 2016 by
Gareth Stevens Publishing
111 East 14th Street, Suite 349
New York, NY 10003

Copyright © 2016 Gareth Stevens Publishing

Designer: Andrea Davison-Bartolotta
Editor: Kristen Rajczak

Photo credits: Cover, p. 1 (right) mundoview/Shutterstock.com; cover, p. 1 (left) Jason Patrick Ross/Shutterstock.com; cover, back cover, interior (background texture) Marilyn Volan/Shutterstock.com; pp. 4, 6, 8, 10, 12, 14, 16, 18, 20 (blue sign) Vitezslav Valka/Shutterstock.com; pp. 4, 6, 8, 10, 12, 14, 16, 18, 20, 21 (road) Renata Novackova/Shutterstock.com; p. 4 (Arizona map) Globe Turner/Shutterstock.com; p. 4 (US map) CashMedia/Shutterstock.com; p. 5 prochasson frederic/Shutterstock.com; p. 6 kojihirano/Shutterstock.com; p. 7 Sumikophoto/Shutterstock.com; p. 9 Bilgin Sasmaz/Anadolu Agency/Getty Images; p. 11 Melissa Farlow/National Geographic/Getty Images; p. 12 Carol Polich Photo Workshops/Lonely Planet Images/Getty Images; p. 13 Eddie Brady/Lonely Planet Images/Getty Images; p. 14 Mark Baldwin/Shutterstock.com; p. 15 (main) Josemaria Toscano/Shutterstock.com; p. 15 (inset) TFoxFoto/Shutterstock.com; p. 16 John Warburton-Lee/AWL Images/Getty Images; p. 17 Pacific Northwest Photo/Shutterstock.com; p. 18 JennyRA/Shutterstock.com; p. 19 Tom Grundy/Shutterstock.com; p. 20 Bachmann Bachmann/F1online/Getty Images; p. 21 (Grand Canyon) Rob van Esch/Shutterstock.com; p. 21 (notebook) 89studio/Shutterstock.com.

All rights reserved. No part of this book may be reproduced in any form without permission in writing from the publisher, except by a reviewer.

Printed in the United States of America

CPSIA compliance information: Batch #CS16GS: For further information contact Gareth Stevens, New York, New York at 1-800-542-2595.

Contents

Words in the glossary appear in **bold** type the first time they are used in the text.

What a Sight!

One of the greatest natural wonders in the United States is the Grand Canyon. Its colorful rock forms are so cool to see—especially seen from the canyon's rim!

Found in northwestern Arizona, the Grand Canyon is 277 miles (446 km) long and between 175 yards (160 m) and 18 miles (29 km) across from rim to rim. It's the major feature of Grand Canyon National Park, which is one of the most visited national parks in the United States.

All About

Grand Canyon National Park

where found: Arizona

year established: 1919 (part became a forest reserve in 1893, then a game preserve in 1906, and a national monument in 1908)

size: 1,904 square miles (4,931 sq km)

number of visitors yearly: nearly 5 million

common wildlife: coyotes, foxes, rabbits, peregrine falcons, bald eagles

common plant life: in the canyon are cactus, yucca, and cottonwoods; on the rim are pine, scrub oak, and sagebrush

major attractions: the north and south rims of the Grand Canyon, Colorado River **rafting**

There's so much to see at Grand Canyon National Park, from wildlife to museum displays.

Pit Stop

A canyon is a deep valley that has high sides and often a stream or river running through it. The Colorado River runs through the Grand Canyon.

Forming the Canyon

The Colorado River doesn't just run through the Grand Canyon—it formed the canyon! The river was able to carve such a deep and steeply sided canyon because it moves very fast and has a great volume of water.

In addition, the river's movement of lots of mud, sand, and stone caused the rock of the canyon to **erode** further. Rain, wind, and big shifts in temperature also helped form the Grand Canyon. All this took about 6 million years.

Grand Canyon National Park is found on the Colorado **Plateau**.

Pit Stop

You can learn all about the **geology** of the Grand Canyon at the park's Yavapai Geology Museum, which includes 3-D models, photographs, and other displays about how the land features formed.

A Place to Explore

The first people to occupy the Grand Canyon area arrived about 12,000 years ago. Places where Paleo-Indians lived have been found in the Grand Canyon. Later, Native American tribes made their homes around and in the Grand Canyon, forming villages beginning around AD 500.

Spanish explorer Francisco Coronado recorded the first European sighting of the Grand Canyon in 1540. As the United States formed and grew, the canyon continued to draw notice. In 1893, part of it became Grand Canyon Forest Reserve.

Pit Stop

Archaeologists have found pots, tools, and other items from early settlements in Grand Canyon National Park.

The Navajo, Havasupai, and Hualapai **reservations** are homes to many Native Americans around the Grand Canyon today and welcome visitors.

An Official Park

In 1906, the forest reserve became a game preserve, or a **protected** place for wildlife. President Theodore Roosevelt named it a national monument in 1908, and, in 1919, Grand Canyon National Park was created nearby.

The park known today formed in 1975 when Marble Canyon National Monument became part of Grand Canyon National Park. Other lands protected by the US government were added, too. Today, Grand Canyon National Park stretches from where Arizona meets Utah to the Grand Wash Cliffs near Nevada.

Pit Stop

Visitors to the Grand Canyon view the canyon by either the south rim or the north rim. Most visitors travel to the south rim because it's easier to get to and is open year-round. The north rim is only open from May 15 to October 15.

The Grand Wash Cliffs are a beautiful sight to see when visiting the park.

Hiker's Dream

Do you love to hike? If so, Grand Canyon National Park is the place for you! There are many miles of hiking trails around and down into the canyon.

Those who are especially adventurous can even hike *across* the Grand Canyon. There's a trail 21 miles (34 km) long that connects the south rim to the north rim. You have to climb down one side of the canyon and up the other! You may also use a footbridge built 70 feet (21 m) above the roaring Colorado River.

hikers on the south rim

For those traveling around the canyon, it's about 220 miles (354 km) from the south rim to the north rim.

Pit Stop

If you're visiting the Grand Canyon during the summer, it's best to hike early in the morning or after about 4 p.m. The middle of the day is very hot and this can be dangerous for hikers.

Rent a Mule

Perhaps the most famous way to see the Grand Canyon is by mule. Some rides are only a few hours. Others take riders to the bottom of the canyon to stay overnight at Phantom Ranch. Mule rides let you see the canyon up close. However, it's a long time in the **saddle**, so riders must be fit and unafraid of being up high.

Hiking and riding in the park can cause problems for people who have heart or breathing problems. The high **elevation** means the air is thin—and that can make even walking hard!

Pit Stop

Mules not for you? Rent a bike and see Grand Canyon National Park on two wheels!

The south rim is about 7,000 feet (2,134 m) above sea level. The north rim is higher, with an average elevation of 8,000 feet (2,438 m).

south rim viewing area

River Rafting

The Colorado River offers many opportunities for fun on a road trip to Grand Canyon National Park. Rafting trips can be 3 days to 3 weeks long! Some of these trips take travelers through white water, or places with **rapids**. "Smooth water" trips are through calmer parts of the river.

When on a rafting trip on the Colorado River, you may carry all your food and water on your back. If the trip is a long one, you'll have to carry your own toilet!

Pit Stop

Trips down the Colorado River may be in boats travelers paddle themselves or in motor-powered boats. You can see the whole canyon this way if you want!

Facing the white water of the Colorado River takes daring rafters!

Enjoy Nature

In Grand Canyon National Park, forests, side canyons, and nearby plateaus make the park much more than just the Grand Canyon. Spot a California condor or bald eagle flying through the sky and enjoy the more than 1,500 kinds of plants and trees in the park.

Take your road trip beyond the park to see more natural beauty. Kaibab National Forest surrounds much of the park. Lake Mead isn't far away, and Zion National Park is only about 100 miles (161 km) away.

Painted Desert

Pit Stop

The Grand Canyon's walls are pink, gray, purple, and many shades of brown from the way the layers of rock formed. In the nearby Painted Desert, visitors can see even more colorful rock!

The Desert View Watchtower is found at the highest point on the south rim and is a popular place for visitors to hike to. It offers great views of Grand Canyon National Park.

Far Out!

Grand Canyon National Park is far from a lot of places, such as stores and gas stations, you're used to having nearby. When visiting, it's important to bring everything you might need, especially water.

The most popular time of year to visit the park is from March to October, and those summer months can be *hot*! However, if you visit in December or January, there could be snow. Whatever the time of year, Grand Canyon National Park is a beautiful stop on a road trip.

Pit Stop

Depending on the spring weather, there's been snow as late as June and freezing temperatures on the north rim in July!

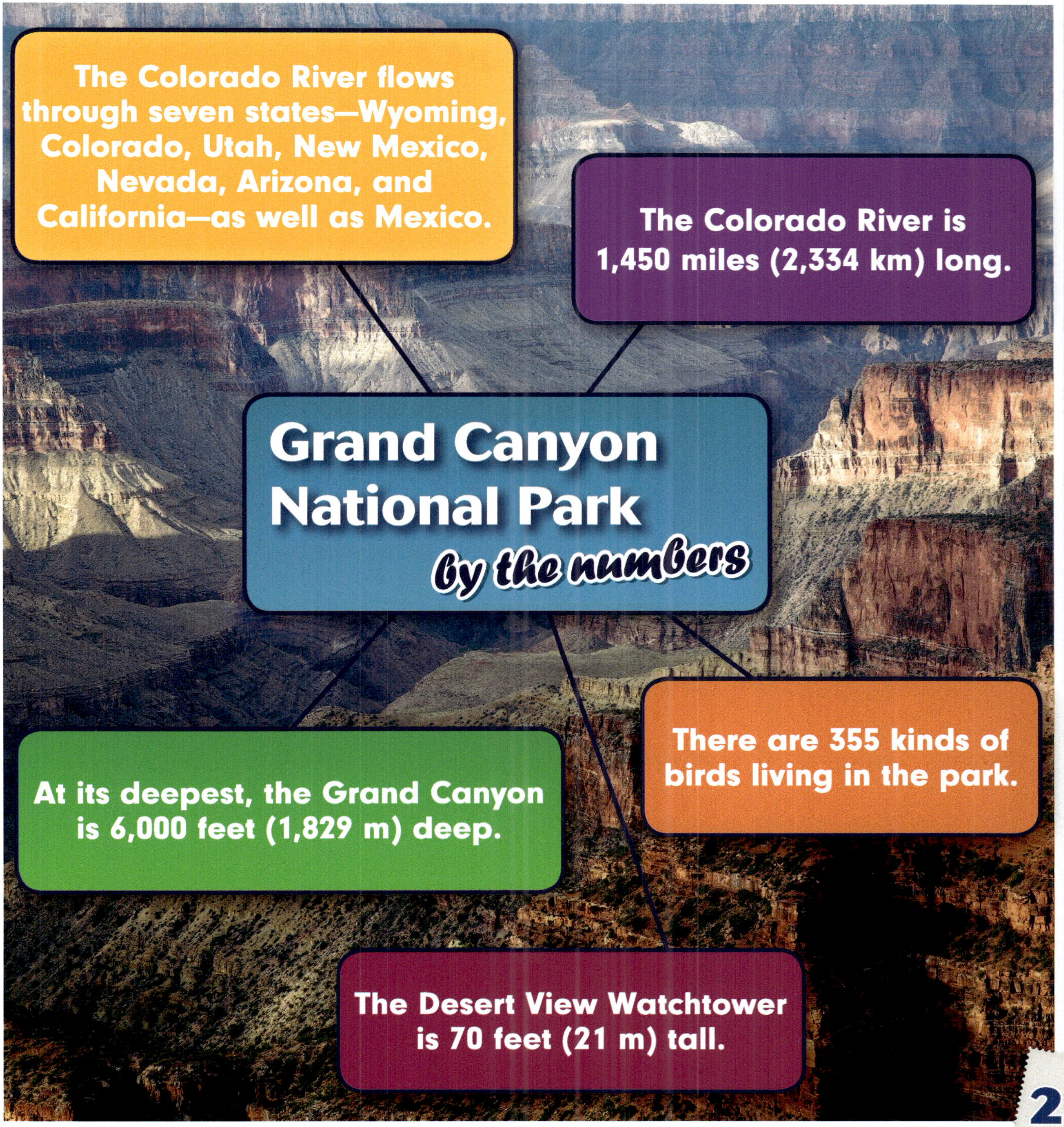

Grand Canyon National Park

by the numbers

The Colorado River flows through seven states—Wyoming, Colorado, Utah, New Mexico, Nevada, Arizona, and California—as well as Mexico.

The Colorado River is 1,450 miles (2,334 km) long.

At its deepest, the Grand Canyon is 6,000 feet (1,829 m) deep.

There are 355 kinds of birds living in the park.

The Desert View Watchtower is 70 feet (21 m) tall.

Glossary

archaeologist: a scientist who studies past human life and activities

elevation: height above sea level

erode: to wear away outer layers of rock or soil by the action of wind and water

geology: the science that studies the history of Earth and its life as recorded in rocks

plateau: a large area of land with raised sides and a level top

protected: kept safe

rafting: traveling in a flat boat with low sides

rapids: a part of a river where the water moves fast and there are rocks

reservation: land set aside by the US government for Native Americans. A reserve is land set aside for wildlife.

saddle: a padded seat used to ride a horse or mule

For More Information

Books

DeFries, Cheryl L. *What Are the 7 Natural Wonders of the United States?* Berkeley Heights, NJ: Enslow Publishers, Inc., 2013.

Frisch, Nate. *Grand Canyon National Park.* Mankato, MN: Creative Education, 2014.

Websites

Grand Canyon Facts for Kids
www.sciencekids.co.nz/sciencefacts/earth/grandcanyon.html
This website gives many interesting facts about the Grand Canyon.

Grand Canyon National Park: For Kids
www.nps.gov/grca/forkids/index.htm
Learn about all the programs offered at Grand Canyon National Park just for kids.

Publisher's note to educators and parents: Our editors have carefully reviewed these websites to ensure that they are suitable for students. Many websites change frequently, however, and we cannot guarantee that a site's future contents will continue to meet our high standards of quality and educational value. Be advised that students should be closely supervised whenever they access the Internet.

Index